YACHT HADIR 2 IN PEACE AND WAR

FREDERICK WALLIS

authorHOUSE®

AuthorHouse™ UK
1663 Liberty Drive
Bloomington, IN 47403 USA
www.authorhouse.co.uk
Phone: 0800.197.4150

Published by AuthorHouse 12/21/2015

ISBN: 978-1-5049-9651-8 (sc)
ISBN: 978-1-5049-9652-5 (e)

THIS STORY REALLY STARTS IN the Munich Crisis, having orders to bring the yacht from Dover, where she was lying in the Bromwell Dock and to bring her home as quickly as possible to Bridlington. With all possible speed, my mate Mr. George Pogson of Cleethorpes and I left for Dover. On arrival at Dover we filled the yacht up with fuel and left for Ramsgate as the tide did not suit for crossing the Thames Estuary. We laid in the outer harbour alongside a dredger; we then turned in until 2am. At the appointed time we left, and with a fair tide crossed the Thames with a then freshly increasing Easterly wind and a quickly rising sea. Fortunately we had partaken of some food before leaving Ramsgate as it proved impossible to keep a kettle on the stove, a drink of water and a biscuit or two had to suffice. Our Wireless was out of order so we had no idea whether the war had been declared or not.

We made good progress North despite the continuous lolling and pitching throughout the night. We were more than pleased when it finally broke daylight which seemed to give us a fresh outlook on life. Our course was to take us over the Yorkshire Hale grounds which we were to cross at 3 o'clock the following afternoon after leaving Dover. It was at this time that one of the strangest things happened, such as I had never experienced before, the yacht suddenly ran out of the extremely bad weather into an absolute great calm, it was incredible! Immediately the kettle was put on the galley stove and we partook of a whacking great meal plus a good pint pot of hot tea.

Then it was time for a good wash and a shave after which we generally tidied and straightened things up, in readiness for our arrival in Bridlington. We still had no news of whether Britain was at war or not.

We arrived at Bridlington on a Saturday night and handed over the yacht to Mr. Bob Usher the owner's caretaker telling him of the strong breeze we had encountered, all the way up to the Yorkshire Hale grounds. Before taking our leave of Mr. Usher we assisted him to put out extra mooring ropes and additional fenders.

The breeze finally reached Bridlington the following day Sunday and numerous local fishing cables plus passengers were caught out in the arousing breeze but fortunately all returned to the harbour safely. So much for the Munich Crisis, Chamberlain had returned with a scrap of paper 'Peace in our time', Baloney!!!

The next time we meet the HADIR 2 was in the early part of 1939. After working on the yacht owner's commercial speed boat with the understanding that I was to take the HADIR 2 as part of the job to Amsterdam. I made arrangements for the mate Mr. G Pogson of Cleethorpes to come to Bridlington in readiness for the forthcoming trip to Amsterdam. Also accompanying us on this voyage was to be a friend of mine Mr. Noel Oxberry on a pleasure basis.

We left Bridlington on a Saturday at 1pm and proceeded down the coast across the Humber and down through the world. Being fine weather we took our course from the St. Nicholas Light Vessel and so to Ymaiden. We arrived at Ymaiden at 6pm on the Sunday night it was blowing hard Southerly and pouring with rain. We locked through into the canal and then moored up alongside the Quay. After we had tea and cleaned up the cabin, we went ashore that night to Wilhelmina's Café and Dance Hall and stayed until 4 o'clock the following morning.

It was still blowing hard and pouring with rain at day break when we then proceeded up to the Amsterdam Yacht Haven. Inside the Yacht Haven were moored two new German sailing yachts with a man and a woman on each as the crew. By now the weather had turned fine, so we spread all our gear out on the grass to dry and gave the yacht a thorough clean up, washing her on the inside and outside, leaving her looking very nice and clean, we then went ashore sightseeing.

I noticed with the German yachts that if the male crew member went ashore with his camera, the female member stayed on board and should the female member go ashore with a camera the male member stayed on board, I thought this very strange at the time. The following morning I was talking to a Dutch Yacht Captain who spoke very good English and his story was that he couldn't see how these German yacht people were managing, because at that time anyone leaving Germany were only allowed to take 60 marks out of the country and apparently these German yachters had been in Amsterdam for a considerable number of weeks doing nothing else but take photographs and surely must have spent thousands of marks, his final words were "We shall be at war with them before long, I can see it coming".

One of the German men used to go ashore each morning for a bath and to get to the baths he had to pass our yacht. He was a very surly man and as he passed by our yacht he used to spit at the Royal Yorkshire Yacht Club Blue Ensign which we were flying. I often think of the Dutch Yacht Captain's words when he called them damned German spies.

Whilst we were sightseeing the Germans were taking photographs of the Air Raid Shelter which were down the middle of the streets. I passed a remark at the time that all the Germans would have to do, would be to drop a leave and bomb down the middle of the street and apparently that was to happen later. We could around for the rest of the week and then left on the associated Humber Lines steamer "Dewsbury" on the Saturday night and arrived at Hull at 1pm Sunday. My friend and I finally arrived in Bridlington at 2.30pm good going we thought.

All during the summer there were rumours of war, and by then in August the takings in the speed boat had hit rock bottom. On seeing the owner of the yacht Hadir 2 I told him that his best plan would be to get his yacht back to England as there was going to be a war, he said 'ridiculous' when he had finished oaring in Holland he had laid his yacht up at De Viers Lenches Shipyard at Glasweg. I finished working with the speedboat and took on a labourer's job at Driffield Aerodrome and I was working there at the outbreak of war. On returning home from work one night in February, my wife told me that Mr. Blakely the owner of the yacht Hadir 2 had been and would I go and see him after tea. I went to see Mr. Blakely wondering what was in the wind, and over a drink he told me that I had been right all the time. He also told me that he had written to the Government to see if he could get permission to bring his yacht from Amsterdam and if he was to be successful would I bring her back to England via the canals of Holland, Belgium and France.

I told him that he ought to have brought his yacht back home after finishing cruising in Holland and that it would be difficult for me to find a mate willing to take on the risks involved, especially as my regular mate from Cleethorpes had been ill for some time. I decided to ask a friend of mine Mr. Robert Ellison who kept a house boat in Bridlington Harbour, he agreed to go with me once and if permission were granted, providing the owner paid for all the necessary passports and visas required. We now had to wait, February passed by and on the

10th March permission was given to fetch the yacht, and that was to be the start of many more adventures for the Hadir 2 and myself, had I known what was to lay in store for me Mr. Blakely would have received back word.

We left Bridlington on the early morning train for Hull where we changed trains for Kings Cross station London arriving at 2.30pm. We booked into the Endsleigh Hotel opposite the Tropical Disease Hospital and stayed overnight. The following morning on the 12th March we took a taxi to Victoria Station where we were met by a Thomas Cook's courier who promptly locked us in a carriage on a non couidas train, which then left for Gravesend. On arrival at Gravesend all the passengers were herded into a waiting room and searched and what with women and children crying the place was like bedlam. We however were taken away and searched separately, what for I shall never know, a parson and his wife even had their bibles taken from them and my friend Bob had an envelope and a sheet of writing paper confiscated. After showing our Admiralty Permit we were segregated from the other passengers.

At 5pm that night the s/s BATAVIA 2 berthed alongside the quay and we thankfully embarked aboard her, glad to be clear of all the chaos and misery experienced in the waiting rooms. The Dutch passenger vessel Batavir 2 eventually left the Quay and proceeded to an anchorage in the Downs for the night. At supper time we met our fellow shipmates for the voyage, most of whom were shipwrecked crews who had been torpedoed, they consisted of many nationalities Danish, Dutch, Hungarian and Japanese. Getting to the bar a good time was had by all until the early hours. The Batavia 2 got under way at first light, everyone was then ordered to put on life belts. As the morning progressed it became warm and sunny and whilst passing the mouth of the Rivera Scheldt we counted 15 floating mines, it seemed odd to see Gulls sitting on top of the mines busily preening their feathers totally unaware of the mines high explosive content. During the afternoon it came in thick with fog and we had to anchor for an hour or so, we were fortunate that it hadn't been poor visibility whilst off the mouth of the Rivera Scheldt; after the fog cleared we proceeded to Rotterdam arriving at 8pm local time.

I asked one of the stewards which was the best place to stay for the night and he recommended the Fritz Hotel, this was to be our first taste of the Germans. After having a meal we decided to go and have a look around the town, making sure that we took all our papers, passports etc. with us, on arriving back at the Hotel we decided to have a wash and going to my bag to take out my toilet gear I noticed that someone had been through my bag, nothing was missing but having packed my bag personally I knew where everything was and how placed. My mate Bob said surely you are mistaken but on looking at his own bag he found that he had suffered similarly. The streets had a covering of 18 inches of snow and every now and then you could hear explosive sounds, they were apparently blowing up the ice in the canals to get them clear for a transhipment of German coal to Italy.

We left Rotterdam on the 14th March at 10am for Amsterdam and on arrival there, we went to the British Consul as ordered. The consul said that he had been expecting us for some time now but we told that our permission had just been granted and we had set off immediately. He gave us a cup of tea and a biscuit and informed us that the Hadir 2 was all ready for leaving and that there were no debts against her, but should we have any trouble then we were to leave the yacht there and report back to him. After thanking him for his hospitality we left for De Viers Lenches of Glasweg.

Taking the free ferry across to the Glasweg side where we struggled through 2 feet of snow and going over the locks it was waist high. We finally got to the office at 5pm, cold, wet and very hungry, I asked for the ships keys and on securing these we went to look her over and did we get a shock. There were engine parts scattered all over the engine room floor, the wash hand basins were all disconnected it was an absolute shambles. Back to the office I went and asked De Viers Lenches as to what was the matter as the British Consul had informed us that the yacht was already for sea, all I received was an evasive answer.

There was 2 feet of snow on her deck and everything inside was either wet or damp, there was no Calor Gas on board at the time so I asked him how we were supposed to keep warm he eventually provided us with an electric fire I don't know whether he wanted to kill us both or not as the fire was faulty and if you touched it you were immediately knocked flat on your back, a proper lash up.

The shipyard front was in a cul-de-sac and at the other side of the cul-de-sac was Antony Fakkers aircraft factory, on-going onto the deck to sweep off the snow we noticed that they were about to load a plane onto a barge but on seeing us watching them, they pushed it back into the shed. That night we checked over the engine and its parts and reassembled it again. The following morning when De Viers Lenches come on to the scene and saw the engine running he nearly went hairless. He demanded to know who had put the engine together again and on being told that we had he said that this ship does not leave Glasweg until there is a £25 paid into the bank. How we were to pay the £25 I don't know as we were only allowed to leave England wit £10 each in currency and quite a lot of this had been used by then, on our food aboard the Batavia 2, The Hotel Fritz, taxi fares in Rotterdam, sail fares and stores etc.. Fortunately we had brought with us some silver money but even then we lost on the exchange rate.

Out of my £10 a telegram had to be sent to Mr. Blakely explaining out situation and if he did not pay the £25 we would not be allowed to leave. The reply I received from Mr. Blakely was that who had ordered me to have £25 of work done. I replied with more of my rapidly disappearing money and told him that if he did not pay the £25 we were packing the job in. I had paid all the fares out of my £10since leaving the Batavir 2 and consequently funds were getting low, for example items paid for where as follows, food on board 9G-50c, taxi to Fritz Hotel 1G-25c, Hotel account 8G-50c, taxi to Rotterdam Station1G, fare to Amsterdam3G-90c, Bus fare 22c, Ferry 22c, Papers 25c, Photographs 2G-60c, Matches 25c, Dinners 1G, ferry 44c, Telegram90c and tram 44c.

The owner finally paid the £25 so now our task was to prepare the ship ready for sailing. We needed visas for Belgium and France so we had to go into Amsterdam, the Belgium visas were easily obtainable an in less than 15 minutes we received them for Gratis, we then applied at the French consulate for visas, they wanted to know where we intended to cross the Maginat line and said that they would have to confiscate our wireless and that we could have it back after the war. I asked them why it was not possible for them to seal our radio up and was told that they would see into it the following day.

On arrival back on board I disconnected the radios aerial and earth thus immobilising it. The following day saw us back at the French Consulate in Amsterdam taking with us a chart to ascertain as to where we were to cross the Maginat Line and also the regulations regarding our radio. After spending 2 hours in the consulate an official came and informed us that we would have to wait a further three quarters of an hour before we were dealt with and suggested that we should go to a café opposite the consulate to wait.

So off we went to the café and ordered 2 beers and 2 pies and whilst the barman was drawing our 2 beers 5 men in trench coats and trilby hats walked into the café, the barman immediately stopped drawing our drinks and clicked his heels and shouted Heil Hitler to which the five men replied. We took our drinks across to a table which had five chairs around it and just across the bar was a large barrel with five smaller barrels around it everything seemed to be in fives. Over the gents door was a picture of the German Strength Through Jay ship the "Columbus" and this appeared in most of the pro German cafes, rather unusual and this particular café being opposite the French Embassy, we wondered why it had been recommended to us.

On our return to the consulate we found that our visas had been granted at considerable cost, and we should have to cross the Maginat Line nearly at the end of our journey. They sent the customs to place a large red seal on our radio the following day and once they had disappeared from view I put the radio back into fare working order.

Next day at 2.15pm we left Glasweg and proceeded to the Frontier which has the largest lock in Holland and bless me, the authorities put us alongside a German tugboat, my mate laughed and said 'you would never believe it', and we were flying the Red Ensign with a golden rose and crown in the fey. I went apt to have a look at the exhaust and some of the tugboats new were stood in a group spitting at our ensign, I happened to have a wrench in my hand at the time and I told the Germans that the next one to spit at our flag would feel the weight of it, finally a Dutch soldier on guard duty came over and stopped the row, we were thankful as it could easily have become quite nasty.

We left the lock and proceeded through the canals until dark, coming across the Ford Motor Works Jetty we asked the caretaker if we could lay alongside for the night and after slipping him a guideline the said yes. There was not much sleep to be had as it was bitterly cold and Alsatian Guard Dogs were hovering all night long. At first light we got underway and proceeded to Wretch, shortly after leaving Fords we came to a road bridge and to our amazement saw a detachment of Cavalry and horse drawn guas and timbers crossing it, I said to Bob my mate 'God help the Dutch if that is what their armour consist of'. Whilst in Utrecht we brought ourselves a pair of wooden clogs each and stuffed them with straw which kept our feet quite warm.

At 7.15am on 22nd March we left Utrecht and locked out, at around 8.30am in the River Lek a 2000 ton barge came alongside the willow bank and began landing hundreds of men and woman, nuns, nurses, we will legions, business men with violin cases and some men with picks and shovels. On the caffrail of the barge was a flag staff flying the Swiss Flag whilst in the centre of the hatches a German flag was displayed on a white flag pole, the flag had six silk tassels on the fly.

We entered the Nord Canal at 11am and stopped at Doordrecht between 12 and 1pm to take on stores. Whilst in Amsterdam we had changed a £5 note and had only received the equivalent of 30/- for it and this was attributed to the collapse of Finland bringing down the value of the Guilder and this had consequently put us short on stores. We left Doordrecht at 1pm and later put into a barge haven called

Zype it was snowing, hailing and bellowing so we laid alongside a Belgian barge for the night. Later during the war there was a battle with 3 boats and MLS. Leaving Zype at 7.30am we encountered very bad weather, sleet, snow and quite a sea sailing through the Hollandches deep the Fishermans Gat and through the most desolate stretch of sandbanks anyone could wish to see.

We entered the South Boland Canal at 11am, we were boarded by the army and police who searched the ship for swords and firearms etc, after checking the ships papers and passports we were allowed to proceed across River Scheldt to Fennizen were we had to await the locks opening at 6pm. Leaving Fennizen at 1am on Easter Sunday we proceeded to the big bridge and lock for Ghent. As we neared the approaches to the Bridge an official signalled us from the quay to go alongside and whilst doing this we ran aground on a mudbank we tried in vain to free the ship from the mud, when a man in a motor driving lorry came along and offered to give us a tow, with our engine going full speed astern and the driving lorry pulling we finally became free after having spent 9 hours aground, so much for trying to save time we arrived at Sans Van Ghent at 12 noon where situated is a large Mental Institution, I remember remarking to Bob that we ought to have been inside there instead of on this trip, we moored alongside a café there and we went ashore for a beer, looking through the café window saw a soldier thumping the deck with a rifle belt everyone was out being a Sunday all the town was there, at the police station they checked our papers and passed us on to the Burgemaster who stamped our passports and said that we could carry on to Ghent.

On arriving at the lock gates at Ghent old Bob had to use the boat hook to prevent to prevent people trying to get aboard for a passage to England, the money would have come in handy but not the passengers, we had to be quite nasty with them. We stayed the night outside of Gent and then left for a little village called Snassherke close to Ostend.

Our French visas were due to expire at midnight on that particular night so we left the yacht in the charge of an old man and then took the bus into Ostend to see the British Consul. The British Consul was most helpful and he put us in touch with the French Consul who happened to be his friend, he granted an extension of 12 hours on our visas and on request gave us a further 24hr extension. We told the British Consul about the happening in the River Leke and apparently the barge had been landing sebaceous. We went shopping in Ostend and then caught the bus back to Snassherke where we stayed the night. We left for Newport at 1.20pm arriving at 3pm, it was blowing hard southernly and pouring with rain, I went ashore to see the lock keeper about going down the River Years to get into the River Geveld and the Farrel Canal where the Maginat Line starts, he said that all the bridges were down on the River Years and that we must use a disused canal at Diximude which we had passed earlier in the day.

Spending the night at Newport we moved on to the locks at Diximude the following morning only to find the lock gate padlocked. On enquiring at an establishment as to who had the keys for the lock, they pointed to a man ploughing in a field a quarter of a mile away. I went to see him and he came and let us into the lock, on the receipt of a 10 Franc note. In the canal were bullrushes as high as the yachts mast, Bob looked at me and said 'of all the places this is the one! What are we going to do is she grounds and we can't get her off.' I said 'that we shall have to leave her and if we cannot get home we will have to join the Belgium Forces, if there is no other way'. After clearing the propeller a number of times we came up to a road bridge with three arches and after a conference with Bob I decided to go through the centre arch which I said would have plenty of stones in the middle of it. Through the centre arch we went at full speed, the ship jumped two or three times as stoned hit the propeller, the noise was horrible – and then on into deeper water we finally arrived at a place called Soatlem at 1pm.

The bridge at Soatlem was closed for the night so we repaired ashore to the tavern for a beer or two and a warmup having little or no heat on board, and the gale was blowing as hard as evil. On the 28th March we left Soatlem at 8.30am in a blinding snow storm and entered the Farrel Canal and onwards to the Belgian-French boarder as we neared the frontier the Belgiums pulled a barge across the canal stopping any further progress, and then the fun started.

On board came a Belgian official and two soldiers demanding the ships papers, passports and mainly the ships log. I had disconnected our radio and he seemed satisfied that it wasn't in working order. The official checked all our papers etc but kept on harping about the ships log book. I told him that we didn't keep one but had he looked at the backhead it was there staring him in the face, we used to write the log on the blank back sheets of our calendar hung on the bulkhead. He gave us back our passports and ships papers and had another look around on deck where we had 20 gallons of oil stowed. Knowing that we would have to pay duty on this oil if it was still there when we entered France, I had nearly finished topping up with oil when there was such a commotion down below.

Ongoing forward where our wash basin was placed the officer had found the case in which

Bob kept his hairbrushes and he demanded the camera that fitted this case also accusing us of photographing the encampments at Biximude, after a long wrangle he let us go out not after more red tape, they took all our magazines, books and even empty beer bottles from us, and so we entered France. At the frontiers were parked some lorries back to back eighteen inches apart and they were transferring items from one lorry to the other, another racket I thought. Going below for a few moments I heard the thumping of rifle butts on the deck heralding the arrival of more customs and police for another load of bull, unfortunately this bull was to last 4 hours, after signing a load of papers, and charging me 90 francs also drinking half a bottle of spirits that I had, had out for the Belgian official they allowed us to cross the Maginat Line at 4.30pm that afternoon.

We arrived at the outskirts of Dunkirk at 5.30pm and knowing that it would take hours of bull plus money we laid here until we received a permit to go into the dock. Requiring some stores we went into Dunkirk called at the Seamans Mission and had a bath and then purchased our stores. We made our way back to the ship calling at various cafes en route and in the last one nearest to ship we were the only customers in the lady who owned the café sold us a dozen eggs and while we were having a last drink, into the café came two huge men who made straight for us and asked in French something about Le Bateau. I stood up to talk to one of them and without any more to do he punched me in the nose which began to bleed badly. On asking him what the game was and that if he wanted any information from us that he had better find someone who spoke English.

One of them left to find an interpreter; there were eggs all over the café floor as I was holding the eggs when he hit me. An interpreter arrived so I asked him the reason for the blow, and he said that detective thought I was going to pull a knife on him, I asked why they wanted to see us and he said they wanted to know who was the Lord or the Count we had brought in the yacht, as we were flying a rose and crown in our ensign, I explained that this was the ensign of the Royal Yorkshire Yacht Club and the only flag we were allowed to fly. I told the detectives that I would report them to the British Consul in the morning and with no apology they left, so did we thankful to get back to our ship, as bad as it was it was our home for the present.

March 29th and 30th was spent trying to get permission to get out of the canal and into the docks. We had two air raid warnings during this time, the old Varne lightship acting as the air raid siren. April 1st was spent with the Authorities, Police and Naval Control, at the cost of 100 francs we received orders to proceed to Boulogne instead of sailing direct from Dunkirk to England. Entering the docks we locked into the basin and laid there the night.

On the morning of April 2nd we left Dunkirk for Boulogne and we were halfway down the piers when the police ordered us back. I went up to the police station where I had a good laugh at the Minister of Justice giving the police a good telling off for bringing us back. Proceeding to sea we saw there was a strong South Westerly wind and a very rough sea outside and when abreast of gravelines a large motor fishing lugger manned by a naval crew started to fire machine guns at us and ordered us to stop.

We have to and we came alongside and with the swell running at the time and down went our guard sails, they took our ships paper and passports and on handing them back to us had the cheek to ask us if we had any fresh butter on board. I said where the hell do you think we had the money to buy butter with, the damned French officials having taken nearly all the money we had. In Dunkirk they had a free tax day for fuel and the fishermen and others took the advantage of fuelling up, we did likewise but a full fuel tank doesn't mean a full belly. The naval ship cleared us and we carried on to Boulogne arriving at 6.15pm April 2nd.

On April 3rd we went to see the British Consul and after explaining our Position asked him if we could telegraph England for some money, no telegrams were allowed and a letter would take too long and he would not advance us any money for food. So off I went to the British Brigade Headquarters to see if they would allow me to send a telegram, no luck there so we were in a poor way, We had a game of football on the beach with some of the troops and I then decided to go and see the naval Consul for routing instructions on our way to the control we had to pass the dock side railway station and upon one of the platforms there a Scottish Church Army man was emptying packets of Mazauattee tea into a tea urn, on looking up he said 'Why the interest' I said that I had never seen any packets of Mazauttee tea since my mother used to send me for them when I was a youngster. He said what are you doing here anyway you are not soldiers, I explained that we had brought this yacht from Amsterdam through three different countries and that we had tried in vain to send a telegram off for money without which we would soon hunger to death. He said that the troops came down from Arras and that they put two meals a day on for them, he told us to bring our mugs, plates etc and join them. I went to the British Consul the next day to try again and he said don't bring anymore bloody yachts whilst I'm here, we sailing from Bridlington and he from Scarborough some chune!!

The weather outside the port was terrible and after two futile attempts to leave where everything aboard that was breakable seemed to brake, I went on board the s/s Monas Queen to see the captain who said that he or one of the master of either the BEN-MY-CHREE on the TYNWALD would let me know when the weather conditions were suitable.

We tried again on April 5th as the weather seemed a little better, more breakages she did everything but loop the loop so return once again we did, luckily in time to catch a troop train coming down the line from Arras and more church army food, things didn't look good for our troops. I think they had begun to retreat from Arras. On April 6th the weather though bad was beginning to improve and on the morning of April 7th with fore and mainsails set we left Boulogne. In our small boat we had stowed two tins of corned beef and two cider bottles full of water, lashed the oars to the seats, the boat wasn't much good but better than nothing. Whilst in the office receiving our routing instructions I noticed that displayed on the office wall was a chart of the Colbart sand bank and that it was mined for the full length of it and on looking at our instructions we were supposed to join a convoy 10 or 12 miles down channel from the bank. After consultation with my mate we decided our shortest route would be to cross the Colbart regardless of miles being of shallow draft we might get away with it.

Across the Colbart we went and on reaching the end at the English side were two trawlers acting as gaurdships and flying the code letter U also pleasing and sounding the letter U which means 'You are standing into danger' however we were now across and that was all that mattered. Passing into a thick mist we lost sight of the gaurdship, at 11.35am we changed our course 51 degrees, it was then I noticed clouds of smoke coming from the after cabin and I thought the ship was on fire on inspection I saw that the changing plant exhaust had broken off from the main exhaust and everything was covered in soot. After closing the cabin door I just managed to get a glimpse of Dover and at 1.15pm we changed course for the Downs Guardship we lowered stowed our sails away and went alongside the gaurdship. They asked the name of our ship, where we were bound and where we were from, and what were our orders. Our original order had been to take the ship to Dover but these had been cancelled in France and we were instructed to contact the Guardship in Downs. After examining our papers he told us to proceed to Ramsgate and we fully expected him to signal ahead and let them know we were on our way. We hoisted the customs flag and made for Ramsgate the tide being well ebbed we had to lay in the outer basin alongside the barge. The customs boarded and cleared us, we hadn't much to clear, and four glasses soon cleared what we had.

After telling the customs of our plight they said they would loan us a pound each until we could get some money on the Monday morning, they also told us that we would require a pass to go ashore and these were obtainable at the naval commanders office. We made a scratch meal from one of the tins of corned beef from the ships boat and some biscuits. Then after getting washed and changed we went ashore with our papers and passports to the commander's office. The commander was sat a large desk and when we were all over the place running around at the double, he lifted his specs from off the bridge of his nose and greeted us with 'what the bloody hell do you two want', where had we come from and how long had we been in port? On informing him that we had cleared customs at 2.15pm he went berserk, his language was even an eye opener for me. Picking up the phone he asked for the Duty officer at the pier entrance and in some very foul language asked why he the port commander had not been informed about this yacht, his words were a bloody strange yacht comes into port from Boulogne and nobody knows or sees it. This yacht could have been loaded with explosives and blown the town to bloody hell! I'll break you for this he told the duty official. Turning to me he said 'are you the skipper', I answered yes and he then said how long did it take you to receive permission to bring this yacht and I replied six month and looking at me fiercely he said yes an it will take you six years to get out of here. I told him that I thought the marine on the gaurdship in the Downs would have signalled us in, blood pressure increasing he said Bloody Marines! He asked for our papers and passports to be laid on his desk and by this time his blood pressure had lowered a little, so I handed him a letter from the Admiralty and told him that he could do what he liked with the yacht, my orders had been to deliver her to the first British port and this had been done and as far as I was concerned my agreement had been fulfilled and completed. He gave us back our paper and made out our passes and off we went to try and get a meal, being Sunday it was very difficult.

As it was just on opening time we entered a big hotel near the dock gates a Youngers House, the first pint tasted marvellous. As we sat at our table enjoying our drink three young chaps came up to our table and said they were Fleet Street reporters and as they had just heard that we had managed to get away from Holland before the Germans over ran it would we give them a story. I declined to give them a story but related the incident with the old commander. One of the men said he was an editor of a naval magazine and he made a sketch depicting the old commander jumping up and down and shaking his fist at us and we on the yacht thumbing our noses at him as we entered port. I said for gods sake don't print that until we get away from Ramsgate. My heart nearly stopped who should be coming towards us but the old

Commander the three young men departed swiftly, I said to Bob 'now for more trouble' he came and looked at us full in the face for a second or two and then said I am going to buy you two a pint for your bloody cheek, saying it was very good of him we the drank his health. Neither of us remembered much about going aboard that night apparently the customs put us to bed and also called us at 11.50am the next morning to go into the inner harbour. While Bob was preparing a meal I went ashore and sent a telegram to the owner requesting money for our fares etc, a reply duly came stating that we were not to proceed until he had seen us and that he would be arriving by car on the Tuesday. When the owner arrived on the Tuesday his first question was how much money had we left, I exploded and said you have the cheek to ask a question like that, we only had £10 each at the start of the trip and we have had to pay out for visas, photos, food, diesel and numerous other items and consequently finishing up nearly starving for days and you ask a daft question like that. I also said that until we reached a proper understanding we were going no further with the ship, our agreement had been to bring the ship to the first British port and this we had done, so our job was finished. He then said that the yacht had to be delivered to Oulton Broods and I want you to take her if you will. I asked the owner how much money he had on him and he replied £15 cash, I said give me £14 and you keep £1, but what if I want a nights lodging on the way back he replied, I pointed out that he was able to obtain credit were I wasn't. Reluctantly he handed over the £14 saying that he hoped that it would last us, had he not advanced us the money we would have packed the job in there and then. Once the owner had left for home I went to the Ships Chandlers to purchase a Thames Estway Chant and was told that I would require a permit for one obtainable from the Naval Commanders office. Having no alternative all I had to go to see the Commander hoping that he would be in better form with himself, luckily a lieutenant happened to be in charge he issued the permit and gave us routing instruction orders that we were to join a North Bound Convoy at 1.30am. I said it was possible for us to go through the House channel to the Tongue Light Vessel, through the West Swim and the gangfleet to

Harwick. He asked how I knew about the House channel and I replied from my years in coasting ships he said we could go that way but we could be taking a risk, no less a risk I replied than joining a convoy at 1.30am, the weather we might meet, no navigation lights and floating mines etc. At 6am 14th April we left Ramsgate for the inside passage to Harwick on reaching the Tongue Light Vessel we lay to let an upward convoy pass and then off we went for the west swim and down to Gunfleet. In the Gunfleet was an Everards and another coaster lay sunk the victims of magnetic mines, it was a barring hat day and great clam. We arrived at the Harwick Gaurdship and we were told to await the naval authorities' permission to enter Harwick, we eventually berthed in Harwick alongside a concrete barge. At 8.50am there came and electric storm with hurricane force winds, the yacht was taking quite a battering alongside the concrete barge and at times the Hadir's sides bulged. I said to Bob that we will have to come out of this and go up to Ipswich, he said that all the bouys were covered up and how were we to see, by this time numerous barrage balloons were on fire and this provided a light similar to daylight. Arriving at Ipsich we were told to report to Naval Control and explain why we had left Harwich this was done and was told to call at Harwich on the way down for routing instructions after having spent the night at Ipswich because of the gale, we received our sailing orders on the 17th April. This told us to go outside of the Whiting Bank miles out of our way. So after rounding the buoy up along the land and made for Lowescroft, along the land the weather had become bad with a strong South Eaterly wind.

On getting alongside H in Lowescroft I heard a voice shout 'where are you for' I replied Oulton Broad's. I recognised the voice belonging to the man who shouted as Mr. Stigles who had been the pilot for the Houestaft Yacht Club. I told him that he could have the job of looking after the yacht if he came up to Oulten Broads with us that I would make the necessary arrangements with the owner that night, he agreed and came on board. Taking the yacht into a small marina we moored close to the Ferry Boat Inn, I went ashore and telephoned the owner and made all the arrangements regarding Mr. Stigles. After we had tea, we washed and shaved and then went ashore to partake of a well earned drink. Next morning we caught the train back to Bridlignton leaving the Hadir 2 swinging at anchor on the Broads. Had I known then that she was to lay across the broads to stop seaplanes from landing in the event of an invasion she would have still been in Holland possibly in German hands. I look all around when I visit the Broads which is quite often but no sign off her can I find she certainly never came back to Bridlington. This is a true story with nothing added.

Signed The Skipper…. Norman. L. Wallis…..
Bridlington East Yorkshire

...were told to come again the next day and to...ing a chart to see where we had to cross

Maginot
...e, the next
...went to the
...ch Embassy
...r standing
...the line of
...ons waiting
...aged to get
...nearly at
...ver time the
...eless set
...to be sealed
...the customs
...t day, I had
...the meantime
...lled off the
...th and other
...s so it
...uld go.
...had now

...coming two days and was told to come

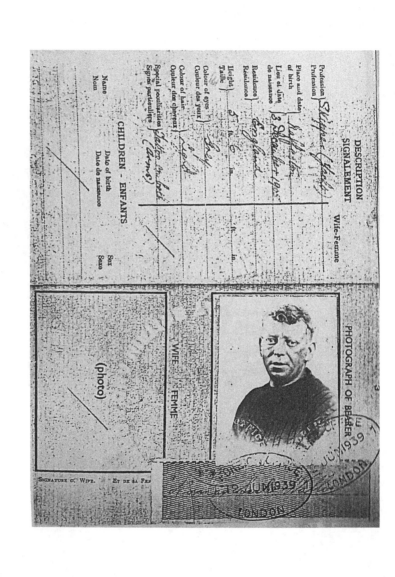

M. Walle   N° 2226
Rosmau Leslie
      VISAS
Consulat de France à Amsterdam

VISA de TRANSIT SANS ARRÊT
Valable jusqu'au 25 Mars 1940
          et de 3.75
Valable pour un seul voyage
motif du voyage Français à
destination de l'Angleterre
Se rend à   Gorel
     en transit par la France
par canal de Furnes à Dunkerque
à Calais
     Fait à Amsterdam
          le 18 mars 1940

[stamp: CONSULAT / AFFAIRES / ÉTRANGÈRES / FRANCE]

Ninian Leslie
          RES VISAS D A M
Permis de circulation et permis M.A.B.
     L'intéressé est autorisé à pénétrer
sur le territoire français avec
le bateau à moteur "HADIR II"
immatriculé à Hull N° 165626
appartenant à Clif George C. Habry
demeurant à Bridlington
à Cliff Oak etc. à circuler par
mer français et l'itinéraire suivant:
Bridlington par le canal Furnes à
Dunkerque et continuation
de Dunkerque à Calais de Calais à Dunkerque
par le canal le plus direct.
     L'intéressé a déclaré avoir à bord
un appareil récepteur de T.S.F. mais
qu'il le fera sceller à la frontière
française. La présente autorisation
tient lieu de permis de circulation
et de permis M.A.B. pour le com-
mandant ainsi qu'au lieu de destination
     Amsterdam, le 17 Mars 1940

Printed in the United States
By Bookmasters